Monarch Butterfly Migration

by Grace Hansen

Abdo
ANIMAL MIGRATION
Kids

abdopublishing.com

Published by Abdo Kids, a division of ABDO, P.O. Box 398166, Minneapolis, Minnesota 55439.

Copyright © 2018 by Abdo Consulting Group, Inc. International copyrights reserved in all countries. No part of this book may be reproduced in any form without written permission from the publisher.

Printed in the United States of America, North Mankato, Minnesota.

052017

092017

 THIS BOOK CONTAINS RECYCLED MATERIALS

Photo Credits: iStock, National Geographic Creative, Shutterstock

Production Contributors: Teddy Borth, Jennie Forsberg, Grace Hansen

Design Contributors: Dorothy Toth, Laura Mitchell

Publisher's Cataloging in Publication Data

Names: Hansen, Grace, author.

Title: Monarch butterfly migration / by Grace Hansen.

Description: Minneapolis, Minnesota : Abdo Kids, 2018 | Series: Animal migration | Includes bibliographical references and index.

Identifiers: LCCN 2016962369 | ISBN 9781532100307 (lib. bdg.) | ISBN 9781532100994 (ebook) | ISBN 9781532101540 (Read-to-me ebook)

Subjects: LCSH: Monarch butterfly--Juvenile literature. | Monarch butterfly migration--Juvenile literature.

Classification: DDC 595.78--dc23

LC record available at http://lccn.loc.gov/2016962369

Table of Contents

Monarch Butterflies

Monarch butterflies can

be found around the world.

A large population lives in

North America.

Monarchs living in the United States and Canada migrate. Some migrate to California, while others fly to Mexico.

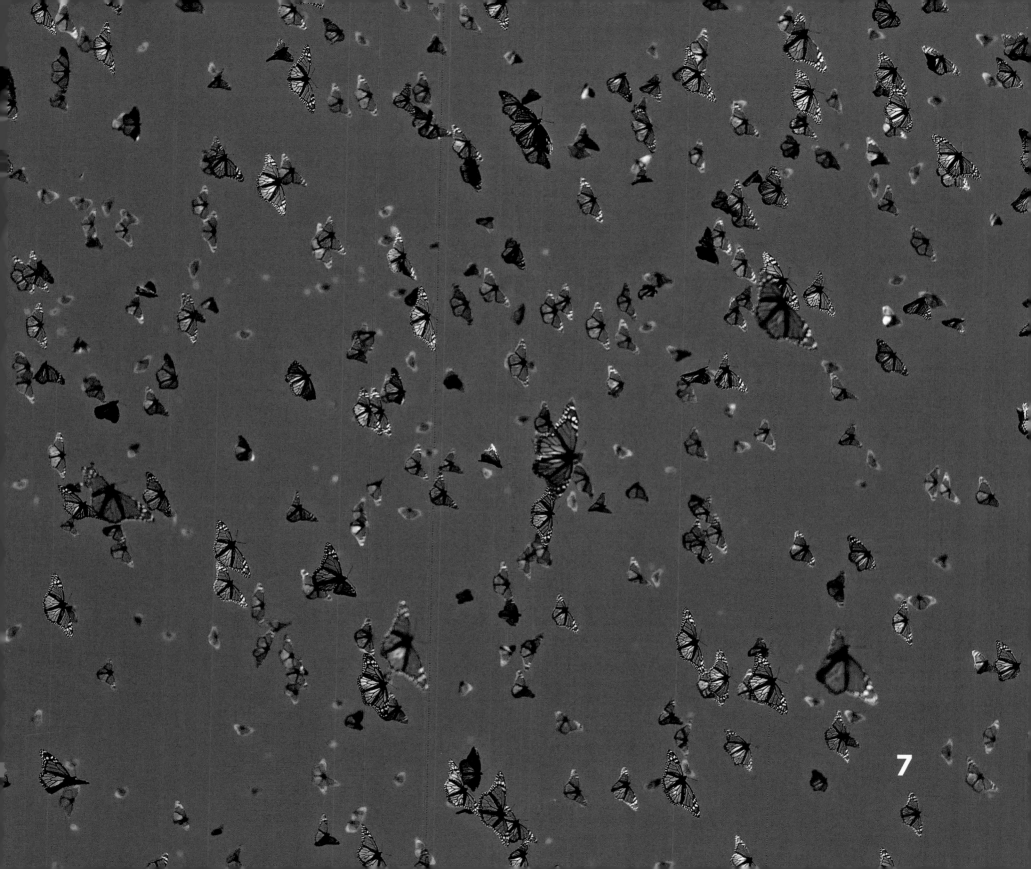

Monarchs migrate south each year. They cannot survive northern winters.

Days get shorter in late summer. The **climate** begins to change. Monarchs can sense these changes. They know it's time to fly.

The Move South

Some monarchs fly as far as 3,000 miles (4,828 km)! They only travel during the day. At night, they **cluster** together in trees.

13

Monarchs from northeastern

United States fly to Mexico.

They **overwinter** in mountains

in southern Mexico.

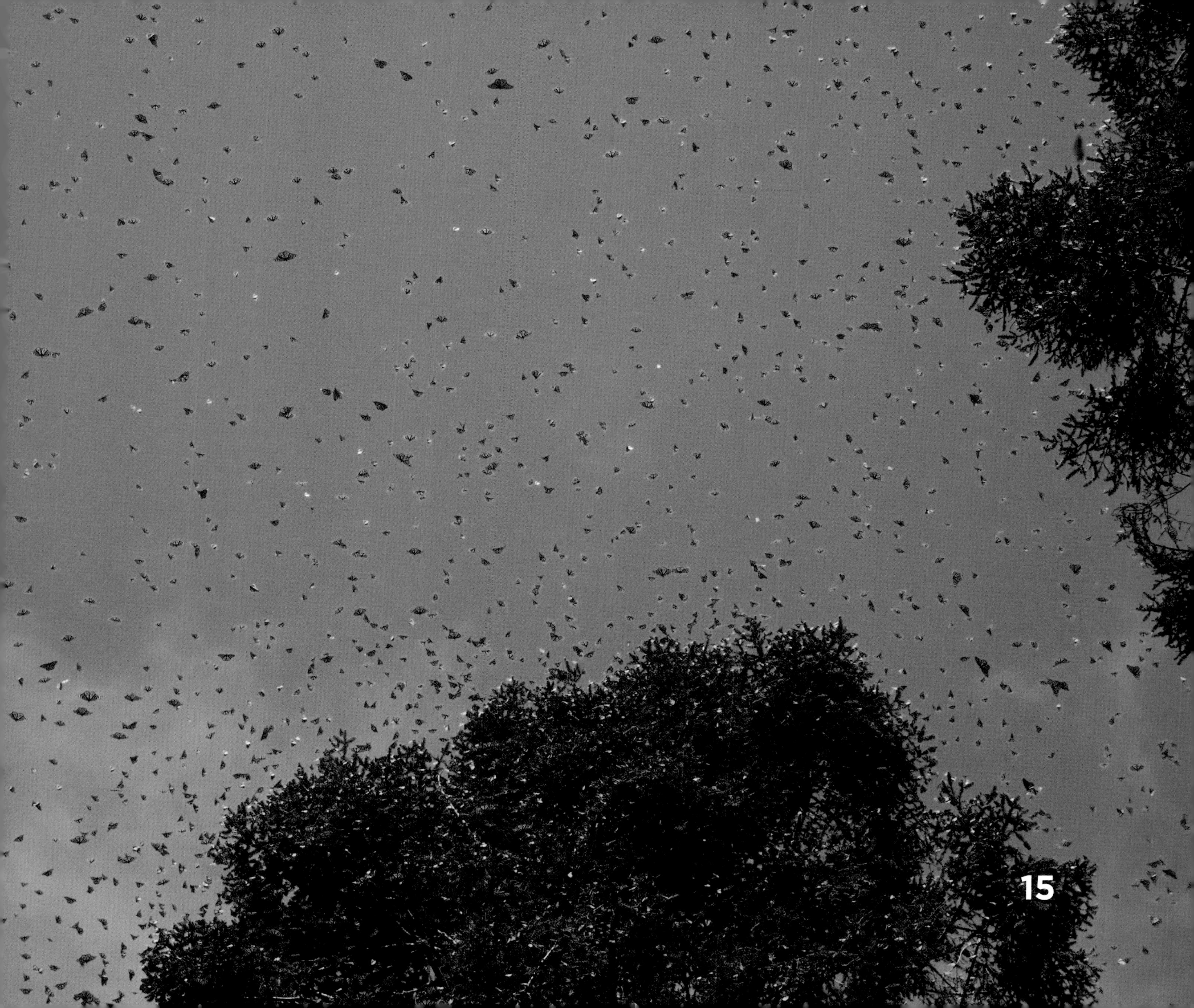

Flying Home

As spring approaches,
monarchs begin the flight
home. Monarchs find places
to rest as they move north.

Monarchs rest where there is **milkweed**. They lay eggs on milkweed. Their **larvae** can only eat this plant.

18

19

When the **larvae** change into butterflies, they will keep flying north. It takes three to four **generations** of butterflies to make it back home.

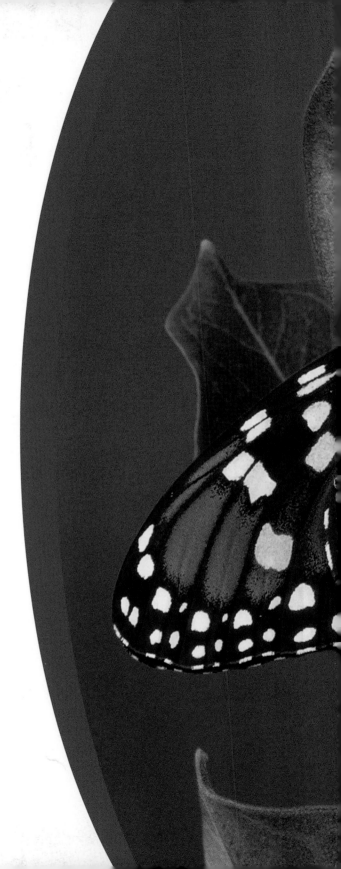

Monarch Butterfly Migration Routes

● **Summary Range** ● **Winter Range** ------▶ **Fall Route** ········▶ **Spring Route**

Glossary

climate – the weather in an area in general or over a long period.

cluster – to form a group.

generation – an entire body of individuals born and living at about the same time.

larvae – butterfly young that look very different from adults (also called caterpillars).

milkweed – an American plant with milky sap.

overwinter – spend the winter.

Index

abdokids.com

Use this code to log on to abdokids.com and access crafts, games, videos and more!

Abdo Kids Code:
AMK0307